ELSEWHERE

ELSEWHERE

NEW AND SELECTED POEMS

STEWART BROWN

PEEPAL TREE

First published in Great Britain in 1999
Peepal Tree Press Ltd
17 King's Avenue
Leeds LS6 1QS

ISBN 1 900715 32 5

CONTENTS

ELSEWHERE

AFRICA

ACKNOWLEDGEMENTS:

Versions of some of these poems were previously published in the following magazines:
Atlanta Review, Bim, Encounter, Kyk-over-al, Jamaica Sunday Gleaner, New Welsh Review, New Poetry, New Voices, Okike, Outposts, People to People, Planet, Poetry Review, Poetry Wales, Samphire, South West Review, Wasafiri, West Africa.

Individual poems were also included in the following collections:
Beasts (Outposts), *Bookmarks* (Catalyst Press), *Lugard's Bridge* (Seren), *Mekin Foolishness* (Trinidad New Voices), *Perfume of Decay* (Poet & Printer), *Specimens* (Sceptre Press), *Zinder* (Poetry Wales Press).

Thanks to Lawrence Scott, Abdulrazak Gurnah and especially Amy Wack, who kept on asking where the new poems were.

For my parents
Ken and Barbara Brown

ELSEWHERE

ELSEWHERE

Somewhere women tire of the shawled sea's
weeping, for the fishermen's dories
still go out. It is blue as peace.

(Derek Walcott. 'Elsewhere' *The Arkansas Testament*)

Grey

Perched here above grey wing above grey cloud
letting windows on grey-blue Atlantic –
the trimmings of my beard shorn for the tropics
grey against the barber's sky-blue cape –
and Michael Aspel in the in-flight magazine
proclaiming 'grey is beautiful'
and the grey-green cabin plastic
bland and reassuring to the grey faced woman
next to me pretending calm
and England's grey, absorbing, self-deceiving balm:
this plane is taking me elsewhere.
I write this in mid-air, between the grey Schweppes
diet lemonade and the plastic headset's piped grey music,
their terminal greys dissolving our descent
into another life, a different spite of shades.

Coup

Coming into Hewanora the four
enormous black guys start to move:

bull necks, baseball caps, the works.
Imagine the scenario; an island coup,

the plane down, confusion, hostages
exchanged for the old men, a few shots.

Someone has to die – just to confirm
that it's for real – some fat, unidentified

tourist slumped on tarmac for the zooms.
Is that the signal, when Big Boy

screws his ear with his forefinger?
The painted hostess screams and swoons,

the Pitons surfacing through cloud
like dolphins breaking Caribbean lace

West Indies, USA

Cruising at thirty thousand feet above the endless green
the islands seem like dice tossed on a casino's baize,
some come up lucky, others not. Puerto Rico takes the pot,
the Dallas of the West Indies, silver linings on the clouds
as we descend are hall-marked, San Juan glitters
like a maverick's gold ring.

                All across the Caribbean
we'd collected terminals – airports are like calling cards,
cultural fingermarks; the hand-written signs at Port-
au-Prince, Piarco's sleazy tourist art, the lethargic
contempt of the baggage boys at 'Vere Bird' in St. Johns...
And now for plush San Juan.

                But the pilot's bland,
you're safe in my hands drawl crackles as we land,
"US regulations demand all passengers not disembarking

at San Juan stay on the plane, I repeat, stay on the plane."
Subtle Uncle Sam, afraid too many desperate blacks
might re-enslave this *I*sland of the free,
might jump the barbed

                    electric fence around 'America's
back yard' and claim that vaunted sanctuary... 'Give me your poor...'
Through toughened, tinted glass the contrasts tantalise;
US patrol cars glide across the shimmering tarmac,
containered baggage trucks unload with fierce efficiency.
So soon we're climbing,

                    low above the pulsing city streets;
galvanised shanties overseen by condominiums
polished Cadillacs shimmying past Rastas with pushcarts
and as we climb, San Juan's fool's glitter calls to mind
the shattered innards of a TV set that's fallen
off the back of a lorry, all painted valves and circuits
the roads like twisted wires,

                    the bright cars, micro-chips
It's sharp and jagged and dangerous, and belonged to someone else.

Whales

Each Christmas they come
white and blubbery from the frozen North,
strange bloated creatures pale as snow
cruising in vast, unnatural shoals.

Whales: the great white whales of myth
and history in all their arrogant splendour.
Flopped ungainly along the sea's edge
or hiding, blistered, under a shadowed palm,

incredibly ugly, somehow, in their difference.
Designated a protected species
they are chauffeured around, pampered like babes
and generally kept in the shade.

Few stay long or leave anything behind
except litter and small hostilities.
'Peace and Love' we tell them –
the government says we must show respect –

so we smile, sing, play Sambo:
secretly long for a black Ahab.

Counter Commentary at Kensington Oval

Against the plummy platitudes
of Chris Martin-Jenkins
on the ball-by-ball, this broad
bare-footed cane cutter,
taking his ease and Cockspur
in the Mitchie Hew...
getting drunker as the day proceeds
offers us all – can't be
restrained from – his loud
counter commentary

*CMJ: And Greenwich is being tied down just at the moment by some tight
bowling from England*

He kaahn handle it?
Why he don' jus handle it?

Good batsman, you g'now,
he ol' but he a good batsman still.

CMJ: And that's a fine piece of fielding by Smith at extra cover…

Proper fieldin', man!
Him put him fut, man,
'e hit the ball like Glory!

CMJ: And one feels now that Richards is just setting himself for the battle to come…

Watchin' that man Richards is a money worth itself, man
Richards is a A class batsman, man…

CMJ: Devon Malcolm was brave, or perhaps foolhardy, enough to say that he thought he had the measure of Richards, we shall see…

Yorker boy, leh go a yorker boy,
that's what you need for he

Crowd e up man, crowd e up,
put all de men around he, behind he,
inside he… Crowd e up!

He flashin at de win'!

Outside de off stump, Glory!

CMJ: What can one say, that's Richard's third six off Malcolm in two overs… The somewhat embarrassing affliction that has been discomforting the great man in recent months* doesn't seem to be troubling him at this moment… or perhaps it is!

Bwoy him arse pain im, him arse pain im HOT!*

Malcolm, know you place when you meet the greatest, boy,
know you place

CMJ: And Malcolm, perhaps in desperation, is showing the ball to the umpire

Ball burs'? Nuttin wrong wid de ball.
The man is joke!

CMJ: One senses that the crowd have mixed feelings towards Small and Malcolm who both have family connections in the West Indies of course...

How the Englishman like black man for so!?
Dey tief Malcolm an' Small man, dey tief dem.
Englishman they like to USE yu till yu dry –
Give back Small de ball man!
He kaan bowl again a'ready? He not a black man?!

CMJ: And he's out, Richards is out trying just one hook too many...

The boy gone!
Yu see Richards get out wid that same hook he hookin'?
Too damn foolishness!

CMJ: What can one say about Richards' dismissal, Trevor, there was no need for him to play that shot at this stage of the innings but I suppose those who live by the sword will often die by it...

I come here fe watch good cricket man
Is not so me come a see.

(* Around the time of this match Viv Richards had been reported as suffering from haemorrhoids.)

Colonial Love Song

Dear Gaynor Howells,* Gaynor Howells
how we love your deep Welsh vowels.
In Georgetown, Fiji, Timbuktu
homesick expats lust after you.

That voice which echoes round the globe
still twangs its Valleys rock and roll
and more than any Oxbridge clone
evokes the green green hills of home.

Oh Gaynor Howells, Gaynor Howells
your every cadence twists our bowels,
like crumpets, roast beef and high tea
your voice evokes a world for we...

*(*Gaynor Howells is a news reader on the BBC World Service)*

On Reduit Beach

1.
The tame St Lucian parrot in the hotel gardens
calls foreday morning.

The beach is empty, just a solitary steward
raking out the sand.

He croons a wan calypso as he works,
mechanically

ignoring the immense horizon and the all-flags-
flying cruise ship

and the schooners bobbing on the morning's swell...
There is nothing to see,

and he has seen it: in the glazed disdain
of the tourists,

in the already knowing eyes of his children,
in the veined

fortunes of the sea almond's leaves that he picks
from the tines of his rake.

2.
That afternoon, among the trees on Reduit,
Kentry, 'Small Boy', maybe just eighteen,

passes on some weed to 'Joe', a tourist,
taking his ease. "No big ting, y'know,

de boy jus mek a likkle deal." But then,
out of the blue it seems, the CIA

unleashed its *Drugs Enforcement Team,*
sent down to teach the locals

'how to keep control'... "Dem say dat im
resis arres, 'e ran, an so dey shoot im

dead dead on the san'. That night two tourists
paid some recompense, worked over

as they walked along the shore.
The *Drugs Enforcement Team*

was sent back home and everything
went hush, blacked off the news.

"The thing too spooky, man, bad story..."
No-one's quite sure what's happening to Joe.

3:
At sunset the iconic
lone, black fisherman,

erect and dignified
despite his rags,

stalking the lace trim
of the sea, casting

his white net on the surf
and hauling it back

indifferently
as the yachts moored

in the bay lap lap lap...
The island rears behind him;

Ladjablès!

Dominoes
(for Andrew Boswell)

That crack of cards on board
is both a slap and a caress
That studied, fierce, disdain
is just a style, a nervousness
That shielding, holding hand
is both a fist and an embrace.
That knocking, knuckled "Pass"
is a confession, a defeat.
That euphoric "Daboda!"
is a conceit, the *coup-de-grace*

Ti Maru

The way they told it was like legend.
This Ti Maru, a one-eyed hop-an-drop
old man, reeking of rum, his mash-mouth twisted
out of speech, appeared one afternoon

unknown and unannounced, to bush
the hill behind the house. Down in the town
they'd sworn this place curse bad, and none would come
to clear the bamboo off the slope

no matter how much cash in hand, "and too
besides" they said "it steep like mountain side,
bush thick as hell!" But the ol' man
just jump right off the deck with his machete

and start to hack, the jungle was reclaiming
back that view developers had charged
such thousands for, but Ti Maru was more
than match for it, he hack and tramp and weave

himself a floor of cut bamboo
to reach the outer stems; he work like frenzy
like he possess, he took no res' for water
or for food. But then the bees swarm, big

and black and fierce, African bees, angry too,
his cutlass mus' a cut their nest right through,
they sting him bad bad, in his face, his mouth,
his hands — and there was nothing we could do,

we couldn't get down there, we couldn't fight
the bees off anyhow. The ol' man he
just roll up in a ball and scream — some ugly noise
like nothin' else you ever heard —

and sob him sobbin' after – we thought he dead
right then an' there but, when they lef' him
finally he body start to crawl towards
the house till we could haul him out.

Then straight we knew him had to dead soon soon,
although we rush him into town, to hospital.
The nurse jus' look at him an' *strups,* could see
she thought him didn't stand a chance.

But when we check next afternoon he gone,
just up and an' lef' that mornin', couldn' bear
to be inside, she said, and *strups* again.
We checked all round the town – till then

we didn't even know his name – but Alphonse
in the rum shop knew, "That's Ti Maru okay,"
when we described him, "he used to go prospecting
in the bush 'round Mon Gimmie. He's live out there

for years, it send him mad folks say.
He was a big man once, whole and strong
and liked his women. No-one seem to know
what happen to his eye, his mouth, his rotten foot,

but he still strong for true. An him can drink,
boy, he come in here one night las' week
an nearly drink us dry, rum boy, jus' straight
white rum. Is then he mus' have heard about

your bush. The boys was sayin', I suppose,
how your place curse, and though he mutter sof',
till then he roar burs' out like thunder
with bad word, say how they don't know what is curse

at all, an' how he livin' in the hills
with every kind a ghost an' spirit an' jumbie t'ing
an they is small boys to fear some ol' woman's
foolishness about your yard. An then he start

to preaching on 'bout visions an' how Death
come by that very morning – like a black cloud
screaming his name, he said – coming to claim him.
So he ran, all hop-an-drop, down into town

to hide an' drink an' make his peace, somehow.
And then he gone..." We left his money with Alphonse,
and some besides, and a message asking him
to please come by. But no-one saw old Ti-Maru again.

The bush engulfs the house on every side.

Jaguar

Tearing the night apart
he purrs through sleeping
villages with eyes blazing.
Jaguar. Slick symbol

of speed and virility,
his ancient twin agonies howl
as they're crashed into gear.
Dread: power restrained.

A sophisticated panther
this assimilated cat
knows his place. He remembers
that the Master had a whip

and is grateful that,
with the grace of his birth
and a little feline corruption,
he escaped the cage

of the jungle for the
wilderness of this rat race.

Happy Hour

1.
It's not skin so much,
there are white St. Lucians
and black Americans
the few Africans,
are more the strangers
here than he:
                    so it's
not skin so much
as costume... the 'tropical'
shorts, the sunglasses,
the garish, floppy,
sugar-bag-waste hat...

The grinning man
who serves his Sundowners
insists there's no
pejorative for *tourist*
in his patois, but still
the surf's fierce hiss
confirms his sense
of being, just,
a welcome, necessary
but still uninvited, guest.

2

"Me, I curse that white ancestor,
Master, short-sighted plantation starter
who brought the blacks from Africa
and spoil paradise for me!
Me, I'd have charge the bastards for the trip!
Imperatives a' history to rass!
If they so miserable here mek them go back
an grow their fuckin sugar cane elsewhere!"

Days

The black lady, in the Union Jack hat,
outside the supermarket, is mad.

She barks and her eyes follow separate
orbits. No-one minds her: she begs

with her hands in unmistakable gestures
and survives. She's been this way

for years, since her pickney was chewed
up by rats in the shack that they used

as a home. They say she left the child alone
four days while she whored with a

Yankee sailor. Her madness is hard to ignore:
she barks and her eyes follow

separate orbits. No-one minds her.

Pirogue Lore

FAMINE AN DROUGHT
FREE MANDELLA
DEAD MEN DON'T COUNT
KOKAKOLA
JAH FORCE
BROTHERS & SISTERS
HOT SAUCE
HEAVY MANNERS
PEACE AN LOVE
DOWNTROD
HEAVEN ABOVE
THANKS GOD
SWEET HARMONY
QUEEN OF THE SEA
SUGAR SUGAR

Colonial Remainders

or the bookseller's irony?
Between *The Black Presence in English Literature*
and *West Indian Poetry,*
Pride and Prejudice and *Notes on Robinson Crusoe.*

Black Lightning

Mabrak was a slave, a cypher
on that blood-stained palimpsest
which is the diaspora's shame,
its chronicle. He bore the marks
of Oyo to his grave in Morant Bay

but, spirit-child, is re-born
once each generation into rage.
His names enact a history.
Today he's doing field-work
for his dissertation: 'Luminary
Emblems in West African Folk
Art.' He has inside information,
so he says.
                    A mystic, (he
hoards the texts on pyromancy,
fulgurites, the loud secrets
of percussion) though he affects
a revolutionary style,
take care you do not cross him,
his temper rides a fragile fuse,
his students named him *Shango*
that is: Dread personified.

Looking for Cuba

Rolled flat by the sea
Crab rocks and slides across the coral,
a burnished, animated icon.

Trapped ocean foams and stutters
                    in the salt pocked reef
Crab silhouettes his brief rebellion,
                    a fist of glistening armour...

The sea swells in
and smashes him off the rocks; from here
you can almost hear the guns.

The Hotel Normandie Pool

It's not Ovid this mid-morning
stretched out on the pool-side deck
in the fickle shade of the Gros Michelle

but Calypso, browning a little more,
luxuriating in her own fascination,
Miss Trinidad...

The pool ripples electronically,
"jet d'eau" the hotel card proclaims
although the shingles are all cracked,

and everywhere the paintwork' s peeling
but Calypso maintains her vigil,
enticing me back, and back,

as if that flight to *home,* elsewhere
would be some kind of curse,
or a betrayal.

Sunset on Paradise

The horizon gobbling the sun
like a zealous communicant

taking the wafer of that Light
and suddenly the world's changed

Paradise filled with shadows
and a chill breeze swirling sand

and salt and debris in our eyes.

And for the fishermen hauling
their nets the ocean's lullaby

becomes a worksong, a blues:
"Days, days, ev'ry one mus' done."

Morning

Bright, purple waking,
nothing grey or sallow
about this Saint's town

on a rum-scarred
morning... Sunlight, squeezed
between bread-fruit

and galvanize, splinters
across the yard. That
transforming lick

of fire, red and raucous
as our rooster,
has changed the world

has opened the eyelids
of affection, turned
this exile to a home.

HOMEWORK

ANCESTORS

1.

One grandfather as solid as the house
he built himself, soft spoken, flat-capped
working man who lived his life in mud
and lime, his delight to make his garden
feed his children and his brickwork rhyme.

Most Saturdays my mum and I
would take the big green Hants and Dorset
bus across the Forest – Totton, Calmore,
Exbury, Hythe... it seemed a distant world away
to Holbury and up the lane to 'Silver Birches',

where grandad's garden stretched away
to the horizon – across the air-raid
shelter that he'd built them underground,
across the bean rows and the flower beds
down to the plum trees where in Autumn –

deaf to all pleas – he'd still climb high high
to bring the ripe fruit down. His one adventure.

Then when my grandmother took ill
he showed another side. Painted murals
on her bedroom wall – sunshine, blue skies,
sylvan scenes. And then the stories started
to emerge – how he'd aspired to be a painter

in his youth – refused the common grind
but tramped the countryside with easel
and a drawing book. Until, they said,
my grandmother had turned his head
and charmed him to responsibilities.

I saw him differently – wondered how he
had really felt about his life – even
if this painting merry rustic scenes
for an old lady who could hardly see
was something else as well as kindness?

After she died he whitewashed all his work
and left the plums to rot up on the trees.

2.
I never knew the other one, a mystery man,
a scoundrel it would seem, ran off
and left my grandma in the lurch with babes to feed.
My father'd never speak of him, there were
no photos and no memories it seemed
except our names suggested Scotland –

Kenneth, Douglas, Stuart, Brown – and my mum
made up the story we believed for years –
of how my namesake uncle, Stuart, aged
just four, died of a fever that his dad
caught on a troopship bringing him home
from the war… And how the guilt and blame

and anguish had just driven him away.
There was enough of truth in this to meet
our childish curiosity – we'd found
our uncle's tiny grave in Fawley churchyard,
all overgrown with weeds, and we could see
how bad that might have made our grandad feel.

The truth was more prosaic – women, drink,
ambition – all the usual cock and bull,
but not a word for wife and babies,
left to make do in the sticks. It looks
idyllic now – the country cottage
miles from anywhere; not then, no light, no cars,

no work that she could do – it was a cruel
abandonment. And then she died and left
my dad to fend as best he could. Eventually
he joined the RAF, Flight Sergeant Brown,
training to fly Lancasters, and found
that his CO, one Squadron Leader Brown,

was a war hero, a cavalcade
of medal ribbons marched across his chest.
And though they never spoke, somehow
my father guessed, says that, despite himself,
he wanted to impress this dapper, Brylcreamed
Scot he found he hated more and more

as time went by. But then the war
took them apart again, for good and all,
"and that's no loss" my father said,
although he keeps the medals the War Office
sent years later in his *Private* box
of sentiments and treasures and his griefs.

GLAD RAGS

Rummaging for old snapshots
through a house no longer *home*
I find Dad's private wardrobe
and discover, like a secret shame,
his stockpile of 'retirement clothes' –

blazers, flannels, shirts and vests,
two pairs of buffed up brogues.
A smart man's hedge against
the grey inflation of his days
into a threadbare dotage.

It is ironic, this late hoarding
to see out a life so blessed
in its bare lack of acquisitions –
no house, no car, and nothing owed.
A life of grime, of beating steel

into a weekly envelope that could,
just, keep his family fed and clothed.
He would not have that pressed
and polished dignity betrayed now
by a pensioned shabbiness

still less leave on that final jaunt
turned out in any but his best.
These furtive, moth-balled glad rags
are his chosen intimates,
his clothes to be seen dead in,

earned and paid for, like the rest.

DEAD MEN'S SHIRTS

Priscilla bought them at a jumble sale
'A bargain really and I knew you wouldn't care...'
Nor do I, really, though can't help imagine
what went on inside these stripes and creases
the last time they were worn.

Knowing what evicted their last tenants
doesn't help, but my dear insists; 'That blue one
had lung cancer, this chap keeled over with a heart attack
and that red check belonged to somebody who disappeared at sea,
they never found the corpse and rumour is he's done a bunk...'

I wear these other lives like armour,
know something of them by their taste in shirts
and there's a smell washed deep into the fabric that persists,
though no one else would notice it.

At first I would hear voices when I pulled them on,
fossil conversations buried in the weft,
could feel resistance to the routine of my dressing,
he buttoned from the bottom, always hung it on a peg,

whereas... I sense resentment sometimes, sometimes mirth,
as if the cloth were in a constant *deja vu,*
remembering how *the other one* had spent like effort
to no particular end, had frittered time away
on things *he* knew were unimportant or mere sham...

I set to tame the shirts, impose my scent under the arms,
adjust the vents, take up a hem, sew name tags along seams,
establishing beyond all doubt that they belong to me.
But hung to dry a wind inflates the contours of their pasts,
reveals that other lives than mine still occupy their threads
our separate characters in conflict, now warping to adhere.

SPLASHES FROM THE CAULDRON
for Ceridwen

Power

Not General Bullyboy strutting his medals
    at masses of school kids with fear in their eyes.
Not President Prayforus grey in his bunker
    nervously tapping the button marked PEACE.
Not the Lords of the Ledgers, their passionate interest
    the debts of the starving, the bonds of the meek.
Not Pope Ayatollah, preaching fat patience
    to millions whose bread is sand mixed with grief.
But those family men, those mild eyed commuters,
    the butchers, the bakers, the frail undertakers,
the husbands, the lovers, all grunters in darkness
whose Man-making spark will illumine oblivion,
struck without knowledge, spent without thought,
that instant of Godliness; shuddering; unleashed.

Positive

The egg has swallowed the moon.

It's taken. Ripening. Coming to fruit.
She's up the spout, in the club,
baking a bun in her oven.
She's generating her own futures,
a stock exchange, originating, incubating,
letting her cells divide and rule.
She's occupied territory, promised lands
Empire of some young potentate
with expansionist plans. And sick.

36

First pee in this tube; shake three times
say the magic words, add a dash of science.
If two brown rings appear in the mirror
CONGRATULATIONS. If you are unhappy, ring...

Squatter's Rites

Urine sample, blood test
pressure checked, heartbeat scanned,
smeared, swabbed, hormone rated,
most conducive diet planned
exercises, bed rest,
sickness, heartburn, swelling hands
conception and delivery dated
smokes and drink made contraband.

The rite of Love: the right to love.
The rite of Passage: the right to dream.
The rite of Blood: the right to be.
The rite of Light: the right to scream.
The rite of Terror: the right to be free.
The rite of Love: the right *to* love.

Scan

The radiographer, a bio-archaeologist,
probes her sonic scalpel through
the pale stratigraphy of your mother's flesh
briefly uncovering you, old-new fossil child,
emerging through the silt of generations
to this tv screen. You have your grandfather's
profile; asleep in his chair at seventy-five
he scans the darkness you're just coming through.
What message do you bring us, little one?

The radiographer jots details on her pad,
evidence, the dusty facts; you are all there.
But as you turn and seem to wave,
sensing a window through birth's amnesia,
I fear the most important truth eludes
her crystal calculations; your signalling
in primal semaphore seemed comic,
a puppet show, prenatal pantomime,
but something stirring in deep memory knows
you're painting pictures in Creation's cave,
terrors from the bio-darkness,
images whose meaning's lost to words, but,
encoded in the DNA like love's ancestral promise;
                              bind.

Quickening

The old wives said, when they felt
that first faint butterfly in the womb
it was the foetus come alive, becoming *quick*
as if before that act of wilfulness,
that first turning over in the crumpled bed
of flesh, the child was *not,* was just
a superior form of grit in a superior oyster,
wombstone, too often tombstone, the Spirit
might bless pearl. We scoff at such simplicities.

Today your mother said she felt you stir.
I go to find your cot up in the attic,
begin to paint your room, she sorts out clothes
and flicks through pages in *The Book of Names,*
our preparations quickening, the tests confirmed.

'Mummy's got a baby in her tummy. . .'
'Did she eat it?'

CannibMum, stirring her cooking pot
of infant stew, bang-belly-calabash
breasts like uglifruit, grunts Afro-Celtic
curses as she stomps the firelight.
She is an awesome sight, a body quite
possessed, replete with mysteries
that creak and gurgle and burn and weep.
Her shadow is a bulbous baobab,
the witches tree: squat, hollow, the gateway
to infinity, a chapel where the spirits
pass from one world to the next. She is taboo,
holy, a sacred shrine men worship at
but may not enter. Her priestesses Death's
midwives, delivering souls into new life.

35 Weeks

*'by now you may be feeling a little uncomfortable and beginning to be
anxious for the waiting to be over...'*

Your whole being is pregnant now, 'lumpish'
grumpy, unable to bend in the middle
but obsessed with things that have crept
into unreachable corners. You are easily tired,
depressed, you creak when you sit down or stand
must eat at unsociable hours. Your feet
begin to swell, you can't climb up the stairs,
when you cough you will wet yourself.
You resent everything – the weather, the street lamps,
the fact that the clocks have gone back an hour,

that the baby books are all written by men
most of all the *un*pregnant, telling you
again and again, 'not long to go now, don't fret,
once it's born you won't remember any of this'.

Heart to Heart

How should I address you, little one, on the eve of your birth?
What can I say that might ease your passage through
        the bloody gates of life?
It is such a short way to travel, the thickness of your mother's flesh
out towards the light, and yet the farthest journey you will make.
I will be waiting for you; the fat, bald, bearded one, looking afraid
and in the way. I will say something conventionally clichéd
and probably cry; do not be ashamed of your old dad so soon.

This is not what I wanted to say. I wanted to talk to you
        seriously, gravely,
in a way that will not be possible tomorrow. Tonight we can speak
of the Mysteries, of the deep truths, of the real meaning of things.
Tomorrow it will be all nappies and baby blues. So, how to begin?
I feel I know you quite well already, like prisoners in adjoining cells
tapping the pipes, we've shaken hands through the womb wall,
and that brief scan, opening the grille, gave me an image to nourish,

to flesh out with the features of your tribe. But I recognise,
of course, that I invent you; I am really talking to myself.
And that is the ultimate Mystery, the deepest truth,
        the real reason why
there is finally nothing to say, except, that I will be waiting for you,
always; at the school gates, outside the party, at the station,
in your triumphs and your griefs. And later, if there's *another place,*
I'll be the fat, bald, bearded one, looking afraid and in the way.

Coming Out

A frightened mare
galloping down cobbled
streets on a stormy night,
your heartbeat fills the room.

Through the open window of the labour ward
the incinerator's smokestack looms.
But we're beyond such omens now,

all our attention focused
on your *coming out*
in that pale blue frock of skin
with its bloody sequins;
our reluctant debutante.

Your mother, floating on 'Inspired Therapy',
launches you into your life's long ball.
You're a sensation! WOW!

And for me, no doubts,
it's love at first sight.
Your card's marked; I'm proud
to be your escort for the early dances.

(This sequence was written knowing it would be set to music by Paul Shallcross. The cantata was first performed at the 1986 Brecon Jazz Festival.)

Graduation

"You'll like big school, you will,
they play football and go swimming
and all your friends have gone already,
just poor old Michael left
in playschool with the babies,
and Mrs Jones is very nice, isn't she?
And they have toys and sand and you'll learn Welsh
and we'll all be so proud of you..."
He knows, he knows.
For a week he won't go out the door,
screams, clings to the furniture,
pulls at our hair, our heart's strings;
no bribe is ever large enough,
no cajoling moves him out of his despair.
Yet part of him does *want* to go,
the part that knows about the things we speak of,
but something deeper, dark,
un-speakable, is being broken,
some bond that will not be restored.
And he knows. He knows.

Vocations

Making haste while the brief sun shines, I rant
and cackle to my class of godless infants,
unable to believe, myself, that knowing
how to multiply anything, even the species,
can be worth all this communal harangue.
Quietly, give-or-take a decibel,
we modern learn the shapes and colours
of our "interactions", but chant

our tables still, each afternoon.
How to spell 'Cup Final' for our diary
and 'pipe-fitter' for *What I Want to Be*
are morning highlights, while princess
is to King and Queen as "swuk"
to cob and pen, or so it would seem.
All this we suffer or impose
according to our size, so that each
may make their way according to their talents,
or at least know enough to survive, outside:
though one of us may never graduate.

Incident from Michael's Diary

(Mike was 8 and could only copy-write, so each morning
he would dictate his diary entry to me...)

I think this woman chucked it away, sir.
Another woman found it and gave it these two men
and they went off and told the p'lice
The baby was just in a plastic bag,
but the bag was all torn
and all its face was battered to death
I think the bulldozer did that,
the bloke just dropped the digger on it Sir.
I was in the woods Sir and I saw the ambulances.
The p'lice went to the bloke what owns the tip.
There was another little live baby
sitting on the boxes, laughing....

Mocks

Hunched and fretful with an hour left
they are hard at it, occasionally just
glancing at the school crest above
the basketball backboard – PERSEVERE –
for inspiration. But for Ian, in the corner,
against the folded cricket nets,
this is a kind of torture. He squirms
and fidgets like a fly caught in a web.
He finished half an hour since,
unable, really, to do more than write
his name. For him all words are meaningless
except as threats: their shapes
just won't keep still down on the page.
His shame becomes frustration
and then rage. In his imagination
he would run amok, overturn the tables,
shred examination papers and line
cringing teachers up against the wall
for execution. He is 'Rambo', 'B.A.'
'SuperIan', one of those heroes
who never even went to school
but always get the money and girls
and are *so* cool. But he's been
schooled into passivity, he knows
the score: Boredom Rules OK.
His restraint deserves a certificate.
By the time the scripts are in
he's rocking like a sprinter on his blocks
poised for the first signal of release
and before the word is out
he's through the door, a spring
uncoiled, howling freedom's praise.

35

Driving home fast, blood pressure still rising,
depressed by the day's indignities,
by minds closed at the age of sweet thirteen

and my furious inability
to crack that sheen of ignorance and swank
reflecting back, distorting back at me

my own capacity for wonder,
like the rainbow in the rear-view mirror,
receding: dissolving; then out of sight.

TALENTS

1

"You put down your pencil, close your eyes, and just think
of anything nice"

Robert's an ace with his numbers
Richard has just learnt to read
Jack's a real star with a football
but Douglas knows how to day-dream

Sally's a whizz at computers
Alice sings 'just like a bird'
Lisa can draw like Rolf Harris
but Douglas knows how to day-dream

Maxwell was sick in assembly
Lenny went up on the stage
Sam got a star for his homework
But Douglas knows how to day-dream

Sally is bored by the story
Sam's quite fed up with the game
Jack got in trouble for talking...
but Douglas knows how to day-dream

2

He finds it hard to catch or kick
or throw a ball; running reduces
him to wheezes. Some nervous link
is missing or turned round, so hand
and eye and impulse won't quite click.

But can he throw a frisbee!
Twisted, spun and flicked up high
he makes it fly, he sets it free
to swoop and glide across the park.
No falconer could ever be

more careful of his charge, prouder
of his cunning, secret art.
Its subtle thermal-surfing stirs
his heart, not just that strange sensation
of control, it's when it falters,

shudders in mid flight, he loves it most,
honouring that broken impetus.
He watches it dissolving like a ghost
in the long grass and dares a smile,
the swagger in his stride a father's boast.

LETTERLAND

"Look, Mum, W for Wicked Water Witch"
my three year old reads the runes of her pasta
"and ticking Tom still holding up the sky"

not just the *Alphabeti* kind –
though that's good fun, scrabble
in tomato sauce, edible haiku –

but everywhere now she sees the signs
of that mysterious scripture
that can bring the daunting "chapter books" alive

and, by its lack, denies her *big girl* status.
A bitten apple reads as "C for Clever Cat"
that rubber ring is Oscar Orange now

and when, sometimes, she gets it wrong
her brother's taunt of "baby, baby, you caaan't reeead"
always ends in tears.

****

But he is several stages on,

reads, now, in running commentary, sauce bottles,
crisp bags, hoardings, condom machines...
reads until the words the letters make

defeat his young vocabulary –
so he invents them, elides beginnings and ends
to make some sense of what he thinks he sees –

"lazy" his mother calls him, urging him to READ!
But he's learning to read between
the lines, the flux that lets words *mean*.

****

Literate, lettered but still lisping
and unable to spell, I sympathise
with their frustrations; feel, some days

the world's a palimpsest of faint orthographies –
as on this beach, now, I strain to read
the elemental signature in the cliff's stratigraphy,

the looping longhand of the sails out in the bay.
Or home, on multicultural city streets,
scuffing through language ankle deep in words

from every alphabet and rare calligraphy.
I live in Letterland: an illuminated Babel;
beautiful, unsayable, meaningless, profound.

from A CORNISH GARDEN
(for Peter Redgrove)

The Webs

Aimless on my morning walks I find the silk targets,
the tree-rings spun in air;
if all such roundels in the garden are stacked upon each other
they form a silver tree, not a birch or willow
but a great silk tree, which you may climb
if you possess the six fingers of a spinner and the guile of Anansi...

A half-breeze rattles the fine webs as a gale whips scaffolding
juddering in silver lengths, in rigid glittering waves;
the dew like broken stitches, like knuckle joints of glass.

Foxgloves

Fireworks for the elderly,
each stem a silent rocket, each speckled cup a flare
climbing graceful away from earth until the green fuse is exhausted,
languidly exploding there in fists of purple energy,
pollen glittering, heady bees fizzing like tracers,
chance butterflies and lady-bugs unstable specks of lustre.

For the elderly and frail
such slow eruptions into fire allow minute excitements to compound,
demand real awe, real contemplation of the mysteries.
Spent stems littering the paths in early autumn
are relics not of one night's brash predictable displays
but, sparking loss, evoke a summer's mute, serene illuminations.

Poppies

1.

Tall schoolgirls shuffling green tunics,
new women budding in tight cups,
they sway distracted in an April storm
uncertain but excited by the urge to love
that swells within each bristling pod.

2.

In scalloped skirts of fibrous leather
May's scarlet ladies flounce
their invitation to The Dance
at every passer-by.
Driven by a lust beyond conceit
their moon mouths seem to sing,
'Again, do it again...'

3.

Old whores slumped waxy on thin shoulders,
red faces smeared with lipstick off its mark
they wilt so sudden in June's smoulder,
discarding bloodied skirts with every breeze
until they're naked, grey and passion free.

Flying Machines

Outside my kitchen window two Cornish sparrows –
tame and dowdy as the climate – play at humming birds,
hover laborious inches over the lawn,
their clipped stub wings designed for soaring more
than playing a tune on the wind; they flap, flap, flap achingly,
precariously perched between earth and sky like ancient aircraft
attempting to fly with balsa-wood, canvas and string.

My memory's window opens on a scene of real humming birds
hanging like bees in the cup of a croton,
banana yellow and Caribbean green, streamlined satellites
flashing between Alamanda and Hibiscus,
tame as the climate; never playing sparrows.

Decorations

Private Gardens dons drab khaki and grey
throughout the Winter, his combat gear,
stoically repulsing battalions of frost,
the gales' rough barrage and a dose of snow.
Such bravery deserves reward.

In January, his first stripes appear,
ribbons of white against a fading tunic.
In February, he receives the Order of Camellia
and bar and bar, pale pastel gongs
adorn his mottled battle dress.

In March, confirmation of the Crocus Cross
leads to promotion; Commander of Primula.
By the Spring, Field Marshall Garden's uniform
is weighed down like a tropic tyrant's,
his scented vanity the perfume of decay.

Traveller

The water-boatman sculls his streamlined skiff across the mirror pool,
it is his function, his *raison d'etre* this movement;
not to get from one bank to the other,
not to make the most efficient use of his superb machinery,

not to come to any conclusions as to the meaning of the journey
or to question its random nature,
the unforeseeable obstructions that will shape its route;
but merely, and that enough,
to scull perfect in morning sunlight across a mirror pool,
taking sustenance where he finds it,
forever alert to the likelihood of sudden extinction.

Penjerick Gardens, Falmouth.

THREE PRAISE SONGS

DB

Sinister. Dark Water. A mother's boy
he turned tail in the womb and shat his praises
on an uninviting world. Yawah!

And how that breech of etiquette
brought all the Docs in Ceridigion
to his mother's screaming bed. A star is born.

So hail this sallow seed of Africa
grown hearty on the heartless Thatcher's crumbs;
already he has seen the world... Brecon,

Bournville, Bridgetown, Bruge, Bayreuth.
Still unimpressed he lives in stories, whether
cheating eight-bit Lemmings or lost in fantaspace

with Titus, Thorin, Mort and Arthur Dent.
En-route to Wapping he's the Cotteridge Star.

KB

Our mistress of the Song and Dance is still,
at heart, 'child of the owner of morning'.
Collecting much praise, she taught the sons
of Oyo to honour their own songs
as now she honours them, in Edgbaston.
Diviner of oracles, soul mate of a bear,
keeper of the elephant with golden turds
she who knows the pathways of Egungun,

she whose wit has kept a thousand scholars
in their chairs… yet she is daunted still, by *Visions*.
Born among Swedes, where guests receive
just "sixteen different kinds of meat, plus zebra"
she's a reluctant raconteur, but jest
about Okuku and she'll speak until tomorrow.

SE

At the age of ten he gave up smoking
and proclaimed himself a wimp. Determined
to disprove it ever since he still,
veteran of too many sad defeats,
stutters to the bowling crease and plays
that telling ball from deep mid-field.
Reluctant outcast of the North's dark wood
his imagination feeds now
on the wastelands of suburbia,
the pleasures of a well mown lawn,
the unexpected joys of being Dad.
Denied that cloth-cap authenticity
he invests in exile's wilder fantasies…
acupuncture, a conservatory,
learning to play the piano at the age of thirty-five.

SOMEONE, NO ONE

Neighbours gathered in the road outside her house,
the kids hadn't turned into school,
someone saw them, through a crack in the curtains,
but no one answered the knocking and calls.

Finally someone broke down the door
and the children were bundled away.
They searched through the house but no one was in there,
it was just like an ordinary day.

They found her outside, strung from a drainpipe,
the rope round a stanchion
that shouldn't have held. Suddenly everyone
wanted to know her, hows and whys and what despair.

Officials came, doctors, a bloke from the paper,
they called the kids' father, her parents were there.
She got all the attention that no one could give her:
by the next day someone had written her poem.

DIRTY LOOKS

Like just so many heifers at a mart
we felt, those greasy punters giving us
the eye as we walked home or to the shops,
cruising slowly round the block in their flash cars
looking out for girlies on the game.
And then they'd stop and call us over, wink
and ask "how much?" and want to know your name,

even school girls in their pleated uniforms.
It got too much, I mean I know the tarts
have got to make ends meet, poor cows, but no one
decent here could walk along the street.
The police "increased surveillance" but did nowt
so all us Mums ganged up an stared 'em out...
a bunch of us just watched the bastards back,

eye to eye, eye for eye, we watched them
to embarrassment and shame. "Vigilantes"
the papers said, some Chief Inspector moaned
about our "taking of the law in our
own hands"... Our hands are clean: squinnying
together's no offence, 'cept witchwork...
I bet we don't clap eyes on them again.

DANCE LIKE A BUTTERFLY, STING LIKE A BEE

'Walcott is the heavyweight of the black poetry game...'

for Anne Walmsley

The hall is full of lights and whites
fat in tuxedos, fanning programmes.
Aficionados, promoters, his fans,
some have paid money, travelled overnight
to see him perform. All goes quiet,
then the hall erupts as the big man enters,
stares at them, hitches his pants in defiance
and goes into the old routine: they stir
up his hatred, his passion, his fire...
He mocks them with unflinching irony
and knocks 'em cold. *Pure Poetry*
the critics write next day, *the Empire's
Champ.* His mandatory eight-counts
punchy rhymes, those subtle feints and glides
endear him to them, they rave about
his muscled form, his stunning imagery.
He is unmoved by their applause,
nurses a pride as bruised as history
by his art's indignities.

HEAD VI (FRANCIS BACON)

The Pope is screaming again, bless him,
his livid cassock glitters as he wails,
it is unseemly to be so distressed, forgive him.
He is obsessed, insists he *is*
The Great White Shaman,
the larynx of an angry god
whose language no one now can comprehend.
The Pope is screaming again, bless him,
his livid cassock glitters as he wails,
it is unseemly to be so distressed; forgive him.

SELF PORTRAIT: FRANCIS BACON

I paint myself on canvas, on canvas
sitting watching myself paint.
In my olive gaberdine worn and heavy
from the rain, it is England
in winter in the fifties. My half-boarded
city bay lets only sallow
winter light, but I sit watching myself
paint myself on canvas
on canvas grand as a king, as a cardinal
even; pompous, pious, crass...
My left hand fondles the razor in my
pocket, there is a pack
of Gossamer and six'n'three in change.
But my image making
makes for optimism. I am more than me
more than double me
in this wet December, watching myself
paint myself on canvas
on canvas, and this is almost enough.

SKY AFTER RAIN
for Jim Malone

The greyness of green, of celadon suffused with fog;
this brittle couplet, vessel and coat,
refines its own un-limitations,
pours through steaming spout
a tradition of love, such eloquence in mud...

sky after rain is our domestic
a functionary we use and dismiss
which is as it should be
for we grow wise in our relations thus,
handling the precious as if it were not;
our words washed in the influence come clean...

The dragonfly motif is a knot of violence;
a deft *un*likeness, as this poem is –
glazing winters when fingers shear
unnoticed till the clay bleeds,
routine discomfort, loneliness,
such mundane bickering as the world requires,
so much unheroic grist

But the pot speaks this, and its obverse –
tea bowls retired to museums, archaeology's mosaic –
is a fist of earth and fire
thrown through generations to this sitting room
where genteel ladies in oriental prints
chime their admiration of the crockery...

(*sky after rain* is the name of an ancient Korean glaze utilised
by a few contemporary potters. In the poem the pot takes the
name of its glaze.)

'SEE-FEELING'

for Ronald Moody

The heart's persistence generates an optimism,
that at the heart of things the known-unknown
defies reduction to the schemes of those
whose minds demand an easy, reasoned order.

The sculptor's green, black, hands confront
anarchies of meaning: in his god eye
the see-feeling disturbs complacency
until the heartwood's genius is disclosed,

holding unknown within known, for those
who know to see and in the seeing, unknow.

WAS-BEETLE

In perfect working order...'
each limb and wing in place,
hairs bristled on the underparts,
this fossil mocks the quick
fantastic creature it portrays
by such stony inactivity.

But what's lost? What fuel
would turn the waiting motors,
set seized bearings on their course?
What lack could be discovered
if this rigoured shell were split?

Was-beetle watches the world emerge,
seems a sweetmeat, pared chocolate
I might devour, suck its answers out
between my teeth, essences
withering tongue like strychnine,
like brilliant scuttling poetry...

FAMOUS POET

is on record, listen to the monster's
scuffed voice grating his poems out;
the angry prayers of a desolate man.
Hunched in the corner of my room he terrifies.

As if from fright the power fails
and in sudden darkness his words trail
awfully into silence, like a dying man,
all energy spent, trying desperately to sing.

BOOKMARK

I fold the pages of my books,
even borrowed ones, to show me
where I am, what I applaud.

My lady disapproves, regards me
as a vandal for such wanton
despoliation, primly resents

the imposition of my hand's trail
through the starched and rustling
skirts of her chaste volumes.

I scoff at this, myself prefer
a used and worldly whore, battered
with love, to precious spinster

forever left unopened on the shelf.

READING AFRICAN POETRY

                              on a train
surging across the wintergreen
post-Christmas paunch of England,
past fields and farms and villages
smug among politely rolling hills
where thoroughbreds are stamping in their coats
and pampered, podgy, shining sheep
grow into better meat,
a decorous landscape
speckled with swans and painted
pleasure boats, and it rains, rains...

It's no surprise these parched, despairing words
seem crude and loud and violent,
no matter how provoked.
Why can't they be restrained,
these noisy Africans, why can't
they hone their anguish into shapes
that don't offend the very page...
So much for poetry!

                        Comfortably
writing my review – for *Planet* –
I pick the few who plump for irony
to praise, some sense of form,
the "writers who display some understanding
of the subtleties their – chosen – language can convey…"
although it's strange these few
have English-sounding names
and seem to hail from RSA –
"who find some other motive
than their rage…"
                              Whom history
and that language has not betrayed.

AFRICA

ZINDER

1.

THE ARMY HAS NO MASTER BUT THE PEOPLE
The signboard blares its sophistry
in the snug black holsters of the border guards,
their French politeness as they strip
our luggage to its embarrassments,
our broken mime inadequate for jokes – (that
this intriguing rubber dome's a Dutch amendment
to colonial correspondence...) – but *Durex*,
like *Coca-Cola*, brooks no frontiers...

and in their Foreign Legion style; the bush Gendarmerie
of cobwebs, mud and broken crates
where l'Inspecteur vets all travellers,
immaculately turned, from gleaming boots to silk cravat,
and so discreet: 'Vous etes Madame ou Mademoiselle?'
he asks, quizzing the ambiguous script
of some tired clerk in Peterborough in nineteen seventy-six.
Above his head the stipulated portrait
of The President – Comrade General, General Comrade –
anyway, a servant of the people, smiling sternly
from his regulation frame among the maps.

2.
Those ubiquitous maps, the leitmotif
of empire, outrageous as their pinks
and blues and greens, or that 'desert yellow'
which dominates these scenes, but is sand
as only the blind can see – polished
meadows of silica. Daubed in dunes
across the endless distance, impasto
but fluid, abstracts certainly, these maps

enact a vain cartographer's wildest
fantasies – to divide and rule a continent
with square and calipers. Whoever
saw such fictions, such arrogance?

3.
But arrogance will have its victories
in the order of things;
        the too spick villages,
a residue of fear in old men's greetings,
roads straight and purposeful as a Brigadier's creases
dissecting horizons north and east
to distant, unimaginable seas.

4.
The camels want no part of them,
lurching morosely from unimaginable places.
Brown as sand, pungent as stockfish,
raucous as a muezzin's call to prayer,
they shamble into the market.

Domesticated to indifference
by an immemorial law; that from
Zinder to Benghazi, from Atar to Omdurman
'master' and 'mastered' have no meaning,
are capricious relations, eroded or reversed
by the Harmattan's demanding fealty.

And so they bear this weight of abuse,
bedsteads, straw, their own manure,
this human show of dominance
among the streets and houses of a human town.
But will remember, and revenge.

Two-toed bag-a-bones
folded against a Saharan storm

like sealed manilla envelopes
bearing the hundredth name of God;
they know their worth, compared
to those pathetic tents of blue and black

huddled like widows, worrying their beads.

5.
But the Tuareg boy crossing
the street to clasp my hand
is not worried, is mad
more like, from the warp
of his gaze above jet *litham*
and the space the townsmen
give him. They gawp
at us, scandalised; lean nomad
and portly Englishman
holding hands in the grouting
of Africa.

What did we say?

Perhaps he spoke of poetry,
the famous epics of Tamahak
or those pictures of God
in the Tassili;
whatever, I did not hear,
mumbling embarrassed in Hampshire
French, feeling my palm
beginning to sweat,
suddenly certain, and frantic
to rinse his dreadful
favour away.

6.

For the leper's embrace is a nightmare borne
by multitudes, they hobble and scuff
to the market like traders; arranging their wounds
as others do fruit, (the ripest up front,
raw, viscid) calling like any vendor
summoning trade... songs old as affliction,
tuneless as grief. Grinning gargoyles
they beg just acknowledgement, the small
tarnished change that clogs up your purse.
'Patron, Patron!' 'Merci Patron!'
A woman without nose creases her head,
the toothless Baba in Fulani sombrero,
straddling a donkey, has no hands and no feet
so waddles his stumps like a marionette
as the dull coins chime in his plate.

7.

In the Banque Internationale Pour l'Afrique
a furtive literary clerk whispers
requests for books in English; 'Achebe,
Soyinka, Armah...' Here where the bookstore
offers only Simenon, Feydeau, Dumas,
the very names are contraband.
                              Those evil
dealers in ideas, smuggling subversion
into quaint 'folklore', seem innocent/
irrelevant enough back where dissent,
if not embraced, at least hammers hard
at the rulers' doors. Self righteously
I make a package filched from everywhere,
stamped EDUCATIONAL, marked
UNSOLICITED GIFT, NO COMMERCIAL VALUE.
Which is all, more or less, the truth.

But the clerk never writes, and no longer
at ease, I fear the interpreters of
his literary wound were not the healers
but that brutalised strong breed
who *know* the road to revolution's laid
by such harmless, passive, beautiful ones
whose fragments of uncowed curiosity
inevitably make things fall apart.

8.

Splendid Sun-birds, Long-claws, Rollers,
they preen and flutter their inordinate plumage
on the painted bulb and palm-starred patio
of a '...better days' hotel. More like shrikes
overheard, their strident calls abrupt
and loveless as their clients' beery passions.

They mob the strutting concierge, who
like a connoisseur selects the lucky ladies
for this evening's contract work, the easiest
of pickings: light skinned strangers
anxious for exotica to gild their travelogues,
or regulars, those silent, sallow men
on week-end passes from uranium.

The remainders, outraged, raucous,
flaunt their disapproval of the clerk,
tease the chosen with tales of pale diseases,
the white man's strange and infamous demands,
but reluctantly drift out to their work
grubbing for coins among the bars and alleyways
transformed by this familiar omission
from spangled ornamentals to brazen scavengers.

9.

Alone in black Zinder Monsieur le Blanc
ensures his grocery's well stocked;
his books are neat, his taxes paid on time,
maintains a cultivated friendship
with the Captain of Police, and bears
the nubile, deft attentions of his
burnished 'native wife' without complaint...

but keeps his petrol tank well charged,
his passport and his francs are close to hand,
has an *arrangement* with AIR FRANCE
his seat is booked and vacant, any time.

10.

For we're all
exiles, strangers, parasites
whose presence itch the scars
of Empire. DEFENSE PHOTOGRAPHIER.
The hilltop barracks' howitzers
trained over the mud-brick town
defend the army from its masters;
knowing how fickle history can be.

The soldiers
read irreverence in our faces;
'Defense de Photographie!' That
painted Hausa wall must be Top Secret,
that quaint square roundabout,
that silent circling kite above the
Restaurant Liberte – 'Defense de Photographie!'
So their power's manifested,
is its blustering tyro sum.

For the market
holds on Thursday as it has
for a thousand years, and the praises
of the tinsmiths are those
their forebears sang; the fakir
and the herbalist depend on ancient laws,
while the hunchback bijou salesman
hawks his images of gods
whose potency's ensconced in the
amnesia of the tribe.

And it's just
five miles out of town to where
the final gardeners prise
their green allotments from the sand,
crop mean, reluctant peppers
and a handful of dry beans;
but *they* attend them constantly,
knowing how swift the desert is
to foreclose on its loans.

SPRINGS AND BALANCES

October brings the grasshoppers, suddenly
sprung into our beds, our tea, our hair, like a plague.
Adolescent lizards, wearying of mindless callisthenics
grow paunchy on a few days of such easy meat,
adept themselves at frisky salterello when need be;
eight-legged, headless, up to their craws in spoil
they saunter into shade for feast and sleep.
But warily, half-eyed: who knows what guise
inevitable retribution may adopt – this compound
once had cats, their smell still haunts its secret corners.

Otherwise the grasshoppers just die, suddenly
in mid flight stoic, stony, pathetically staid maquettes.
They must all die of heart attacks, some main spring overwound.
So they go out as they came in, and lived,
an arbitrary launch into unknown, anarchistic astronauts –
though that implies free will – perhaps more like
those heathen captives of the true god's knights
made reluctant missiles for their blessed mangonels,
the original doodlebugs, screaming as they fell
among awestruck comrades or exploded on to granite battlements.

Their polished corpses litter the yard, suddenly
so much jumble these superbly tailored suits
are tossed away with all the other spent containers,
except for my few *specimens*, laid out on a sheet of paper
like disaster victims waiting to be identified.
They look so stern; this a museum Samuri,
this a folded Bishop taken at his prayers,
and this dun, graveolent beast that must be near a locust
recalling nothing so much, in shape and attitude,
as a Lancaster bomber, standing by, at some wartime aerodrome.

Paralysed to artifice these hollow vessels suddenly
turn metaphors; *being* pared to resemblances.
They remind, remind, of a grandmother struck
through her broad soft heart to a kind of imbecility,
her only and inexorable chant, 'I come I go, I come I go.'
Of the small boy dragged from the sports club pool,
bearded with foam and his lungs black blood,
nor prayers nor respirator could revive him.
Of a history master's virulent aside –
'Statistically one of you morons should have died

before the rest of you get to twenty-five.' Suddenly
Paul, in a head-on crash had obliged. And yet
in those few hours flung between absence and infinity
the grasshoppers must have multiplied, bred
another crop of 'lastic legs' as the children call them,
for next year's springs and balances.
And that, maybe, should reassure us, my grandmother's
exasperated chorus merely a statement of fact;
'I come I go, I come I go...' as
October brings the grasshoppers, suddenly.

CRICKET AT KANO

Cerulean and jet, the Tuareg
from the Sahel with his bow and arrow
stalks the dusty outfield
which is his heritage, his history,
like a wraith in some Gothic drama,

squats at deep mid-wicket
to watch the strange *baturé* ritual,
the inexplicable dances
of the white men in their bleached
ceremonial robes.

Soon play continues,
the intruding spectator ignored,
merely a local hazard
like the gully-oak at Broadhurst
or the boundary stream at Brook,

and with eyes closed, behind
mosquito screens, the pavilion's
ceiling fans rustling an artificial breeze,
the sounds of leather on willow,
of 'come one', 'no, wait',

and 'How-was-that-umpire!?'
appeal to racial memories,
recall the ancestors and holy places
of the tribe's formation...
Canterbury, Lords, the County Ground at York.

Such meditation would explain
our dancing to the nomad from Niger,
but neither he nor we will probe
beneath the fictions that our eyes create,
our shared humanity obscured

by vocabularies of such conflict
that their lexicon is silence.
So, at stumps, nomad and exile
pursue their disparate paths,
amicably separate, rooted in certainties

centuries old, our rootlessness
a fragile bond that will not bear embrace.

COHERENT DELIRIUM

The Muezzin wails the al-Zuhar.
Obsessed by immortality's odoriferous jelly
the faithful bury their heads in the sand
and drone their ritual pieties.
The honey glows warm and sludging
from the comb like thick whiskey,
and there are drowned bees
jewelling the malt –
resonating sugar-fossils
whose brains are crystal libraries
of that sweet witch-angel oratory
the Structuralists can't fit
among their 'discourses of meaning'
but which makes the bee-keeper grin
like a lunatic
and refuse to take my money.
'Zuma! Zuma!' he exclaims,
gesturing wildly at the dribbling gourds
where fizzing bees recite ecstatic cantos
among the blood and dust and excrement
of this profane reality...
An illusion, no doubt,
but one explicable only
in that delirious vernacular of dream.

(The title is one of Lévi-Strauss's definitions of poetry.)

SHADE

'Comparative darkness (and usu. coolness) caused
by interception of light (and usu. heat) rays.' (C.O.D.)

Oh Oxford definitions; a phone-call
to that science chap to check
the technicalities with memories
of rivers draped by green and listless
willows, of languid picnics
canvas screened against the blaze
of August afternoons...

    Shade:
such scarce resource, tangible
as gold and just as prized,
that folk invest their lives in it,
spend energy and time on its fruition,
such ambition as they'd own
residing in the compass of its stain.
It is a pension for their dotage
or a dowry for their young.

And where vocabulary's lyric,
its 'inuwa', a cooling praise
across the tongue which means;
'A sanctuary against marauding Sun...'
For Shade resists his crude advances,
folds her skirts against her knees
as he rides by. Demure hadjia,
as evening falls she *may* exchange
her purdah's wrapper for that
transparent silk your Oxford men define.

CHAMELEON

Stepping as strangely in and out of sight
as a dinosaur might, through some freak time warp,
appear for an instant behind deck chairs
in Hyde Park, Chameleon dissolves
from laterite to tar on the steaming road,
rocks sedately like an ageing Teddy boy
dressed up to impersonate his youth spent
cultivating fashions now, improbably,
back in style; he blends with the teenage crowd,
waved hair brushed back and a-shine,
winkle-pickers, Elvis suit, the bootlace tie,
he remembers how to jive...
so only chance – or knowing where to look
for those tell-tale creases, bags under the eyes –
will reveal him to you, for no photographs
survive of Chameleon, though plenty
of his habitat, ambiguously captioned.

Here, an emblem for the Fellowship of Thieves,
house-breakers, shop-lifters, pickpockets, frauds,
all prosper by his turncoat patronage,
insured against indignities like stoning
or the noose by amulets immersed
in his most intimate secretions –
the essences of daylight robbery;
if you should find one, it's a fake.
For on this continent of broken shrines
Chameleon eschews the limelight
to survive. Self-effacing pragmatist,
laser statesman in a prismatic tie,
there! there! picking his way between the lies.

LEGISLATORS

'There is nothing evil about apartheid;
as the poet said, "Good fences make good neighbours"...'

The President is clearly a man of culture,
he knows the poets have all the real power
their words have a way of twisting truth around
that's why so many books – and poets – are banned,
in case the walls come tumbling down.

CHRISTMAS IN THE SAHEL
(for Tim Holiday)

I.

Among the lush green pot plants
of this chic pavement café
the diners in their paper hats
tug wishbones over Beaujolais,
invoke a prosperous New Year.
Full of the season, they
intend no harm to anyone.
Nor do the beggars – refugees
from drought – peering meekly
through that iron grille
the manager claims keeps stray
dogs out. They're not resentful,
that would be to doubt;
Allah ordered the world thus,
has his reasons, will provide...
And besides, although the signs
proclaim that ALL ARE EQUAL
BEFORE THE NEW REGIME
these faded curiosities
now fumbling their napkin rings
inspire neither anger nor
ambition. Rather, like the crowds
that swelled those Freak Shows
of another life, almost despite
themselves, the beggars feast
upon our strange display.

2.

Spilling from sacks and calabashes
this cruel consolation crop,
crystalline sweetmeats, nutritious
as sand... The locusts glister
in the Christmas morning glare
like high class *novelties*,
our grim, embarrassed platitudes
just mottoes for despair.

3.

Suddenly homesick for Eric
Morecambe and the Queen, that festal
carping at commercialism
and molasses nostalgia,
we drive down to the Niger –
such exotic distractions –
but it just calls to mind poor Lander
and his obelisk in Truro,
where, at low water, the river
shrivels to a brackish eel
twisting frantic through the silt
of two hundred years. Which was all
of rivers his boyhood saw
and that postcard estuary
between Pendennis and St. Mawes
his delta, a confluence
for streams a cat could jump across.

And yet he was obsessed by this
black goddess, by the idea
of her glistering fecundity,
languidly seeping the desert green
a thousand miles from a shore.

His journals seem mythology,
he might have been an Argonaut
though of an age to know
great-grandfather. A liberal
for his times, he died, so his
companions said, 'a victim
of too great a confidence
in the natives'. Some took him
for a living god, the rest
reviled him as a parchment
wraith from Doom.
       The heirs to such
ambivalent distrust, we are
explorers only in our distance
from old certainties, liberals
in our harrowed innocence.
How thorny Lander would despise
our air-conditioned bedrooms
and our cars, the guided tours
round scrawny wildlife parks;
an Africa viewed through windows,
fierce as Tunbridge Wells.
       Reduced
to tearful petulance we play
Pooh-sticks with the Niger, invoke
the talismans of childhood
in this strange and dusty outpost
of the Hundred Aker Wood.

FULANI BEDS

They are an art, these squat grey rafts
of seasoned reeds and camel leather,
a mystery of guile and craft
born of discomfort's ingenuity:

so light-weight that a camel
will take two upon its hump
without complaint, and supple,
to embrace a nomad's blasted form.

But sturdy; stern enough to bear
the stress and straining
of love's cumbersome exertions,
the bloody concatenations of a birth

or, upturned, to steer its owner
on his final striding dream
out to that unmarked mourning ground,
      and God.

LUGARD'S BRIDGE

'Africa beyond reach, imaginary continent'

(for Abdulrazak Gurnah)

I

'Take up the White Man's Burden –
*   and reap his old reward:*
The blame of those ye better,
*   the hate of those ye guard.'*

Austere amid the chaos
of a formal garden run to bush
(its ornate web of borders, beds
and secret ways laid out by some
despairing topee'd nurseryman,
his last barricade
against the fatal lethargy of exile)
the sturdy grey suspension bridge
commissioned for Zungeru
that dislocated elbow of the Empire
where pink, perspiring ADOs –
fit and spick but lacking means,
and not *too* bright, blues
and lower seconds were just right –
were disembarked and rested,
'to acclimatise' or so the Form Book said
but really to replace that pap
the desk boys and politicos
had stuffed them with in Blighty
by initiation
in those rugged, esoteric arts
that really kept the flag aloft
in Lugard's gritty Emirate.
And then the real set-off

with bearers, Bible and ammunition belts
across the bridge and north
towards those mud-walled towns
whose dusty trade routes stitched
the fraying hem of the Sahara –
Kano, Katsina, Sokoto.
Romantic names which veiled
a life too enervating for romance;
that savage, unforgiving sun
or bristling, fevered Harmattan –
the tropics' *cold* when painted lizards
slow to stones grey as sunlight
through the emery air, and boys
turn old, white-headed wise.
Oh how the pale 'first-timer' yearned
for green and frost and marmalade
but felt himself always on parade,
emissary of a culture
and exemplar of a creed
the natives were to judge by *him*,
for once across that bridge
he was the King and they his fickle
unenamoured folk, so many
and so far between the outposts
of gentility.
          So, as Lugard taught,
discretion proved the better part
of conquest; patronise the Emirs,
cultivate their tongues,
insinuate their ways with medicine
and education. Such coy
dissembling was a liberal art;
good men at heart
the DOs meant no harm,
were just the pages of a history
whose evil lay beyond

their honest understanding.
What could be wrong with Shakespeare
quinine and the Trinity?
Deceived by duty and a simple code
they were the heirs to a mythology
whose pantheon sustained
the grand delusions of a continent:
Livingstone, Barth, Rene Caillie,
'discoverers' of a geography
whose peoples had discovered Life
and named its fiercest mysteries,
but lacking rifles
and a sufficient greed
revealed themselves as
'helpless, childlike, inarticulate folk'
desperately in need
of decent – British – government.

So good Sir Fred
that 'mean and spiteful malcontent'
handy with mules and dervishes
was sent to bridge the great divide
between such cultured innocence
and *real* life
by demonstrations of the Maxim Gun
and smoky magic-lantern slides.
But first the fun;
to pacify those turbulent, ungrateful, few
who would not see the logic
of Colonial Rule. Emirs who swore
they'd perish with a slave
between their jaws before obey
some namby-pamby white man's law;
the Holy King of Sokoto
avowed, 'twixt Lugard and Mohammed's sons
no dealings except war!'

No fool, Lugard declared
he had no quarrel with the teeming folk,
only their *alien* Emirate.
Indeed, he came, he said,
to liberate the people from oppression
fear and slavery... and by such lights
proceeded to extinguish those
of any who demurred
as tyrants, rebels or fanatic fools.
All this, his modest wife could boast,
in service of 'The Great Ideal...
an Empire to secure the world,
ruled by its finest race.'

II

'leaning on an oilbean,
lost in your legend.'

And this less than a life ago:
the old man sprawling on his cardboard rug
outside the Post Office in Kano,
tying packages with wax and string
for, it might be, some pink, perspiring
expert from the University
as DC 10s scream overhead
and the roads choke on their daily bread
of Mammy Wagons, Five-Oh-Fours,
Vespas, 'Flying Pigeons', sheep,
camel trains and wailing armoured cars,
will sing of what he saw then
as a boy behind the blood-caked walls
of a fortress any fool could see
was quite impregnable,
of how they mocked at Lugard's crew
of wilting, whitening Yorubas

until his crude machine-guns slewed
the rearing rainbow wave
of legendary horsemen
to a bloodied and despairing spume
spattering the news of Kano's shame
to every dusty town between
the A and F in AFRICA.

And as he deftly twists and knots
the loose ends of his story
the old man bides his time and spits,
knows how the heresy *impatience*
chops at every white man's soul,
knows too, by heart, their still enforced
Strict Postal Regulations
and that notwithstanding sellotape
and satellite communications
no package leaves this office
he's not honoured with his thumb.

And true to type the expert squirms,
biting on his tongue;
he means no harm, a missionary
of technology or plain merchant
of the Word, enticed by curiosity
and a salaried compassion;
'An African experience'
and 'my dues to the Third World...'
Another plank in Lugard's Bridge
suspended now between
the pacotile of PROGRESS
and the trade in new antiques –
'See how this juju real, Masta,
you want buy dirty bronze...?'
between such arts of darkness
and the video elite.

He could not hide his disillusion;
where were the painted tribes, the drums,
the witchdoctors and gods
who cursed in elemental tongues?
No cosy camp-fire soirées
where Tradition's fables hummed?
Which steaming bush of ghosts
concealed Picasso's D'Avignon? Come on,
where were the cannibals, les
sauvages, the truly Africans?

Was Africa this stinking slum
of mud and rust and excrement
congealing between worlds?
This raucous brutal Limbo
where the lepers dodge Mercedes
and *Sweet Destiny's* unfurled
round every 'ghastly accident'.
Where Mammy Wagon lions roar
'NO CONDITION IS PERMANENT'
to the meek on Ayatolah Street
while children, blind or limbless,
scuff calloused stumps and hearts
among the charitable hub-caps, pleading 'Love'.
Where soaring glass-walled Ministries
encrust with clerks and bureaucrats
all polishing their vanities;
the Mallams Next-Tomorrow
and Alhajis Not-on-Seat.
Where cockroached *People's Clinics*
clot with every 'ten percent' machine
that flashes, hums or laser beams
but the sick must bring a mattress
and at least one change of blood.
Where bloated Marxcyst Governors
perform their Highlife antics

to the heart-beat of corruption
pulsed on empty oil drums.
Where God sold out to Mammon, so
InshaAllah: His will be done.

Of course the grey old-timers at the Club
are not surprised....
                        'Foresaw it all
dear boy, and told the clowns in Whitehall
at the time. The natives just weren't ready –
not their fault, really; though the country
is a shambles now, as you've observed.
Damn me, I'm *not* one of your Joberg Nazis
(though they at least maintain some order
still – things run to time – or so I've heard...)
but the plain fact is these jumped-up clerks
and messengers who rule the,
                        so-called, Ministries –
for all their *dash* and their chauffered Mercs –
they really couldn't organise a piss up
in a brewery, and that's the rub,
they just don't quite have what it takes, up top.'

So he'd kept clear of them at first
but as adventure shrivelled to frustration
he could feel the knowing nod, that cynic smirk
when some 'young innocent' fresh off the plane
unleashed another Guardian-smug outburst
against 'immoral multi-national corporations'
becoming just routine, a reflex,
like that dismissive shrug and wave aside
of beggars – cripples, sick, insane –
who festered, wailing round each parking car
alert for any token of contrition.

He was ashamed to face such shades of grey
within himself until that melancholy
Kano'd day his Alabama-black colleague –
a disenchanted Panther – leaving, swore
'Thank God for Slavery!' and he was freed,
forgiven the corruption of his own race memories,
the psycho-archaeology of *his* tribe.
He could concede the secret meaning
of his schizophrenic dream – that every
well intentioned Schweitzer nursed
his atavistic Kurtz beneath the skin.

III

'LEFT HAND, GO SLOW, OH GOD HELP US'

But old ways die hard:
'the Ibos still chop man'
our Hausa landlord warns
and so reveals the forbears
of the chef whose menu offers
'Lank Cashier Hotpot'.
'And I quote, though not quite
in the author's words...'
Language Rules, UK
the whispered codicil of Empire
still insinuates the deference
of tongue-tied natives
to the rhetoric of true born Englishmen.
Confirmed in *our* inheritance
we are invited, please,
to lecture *them* on 'English
as a Catalyst of National Unity'
and mock the patriotic upstart

who suggests a Federal Tongue
composed, so tactfully, of Hausa nouns
Ibo verbs and Yoruba adjectives,
'and all those little words
can come from all the other tribes...'
Our laughter is a creaking board
on Lugard's Bridge, that relic
of an arrogance the world thought
it outgrew, enshrined within
these formal gardens (which,
abandoned to their instincts,
have resumed that lush
impenetrable darkness
tradition has bequeathed on our
'Imaginary Continent')
by sycophantic been-tos
grateful for Colonial Scholarships:
'In tribute to the founder of Nigeria'.
A monument to WAWA's irony
it spans a backwater the sheep
who use it now — still none too bright —
could step across to reach those islands
where old Lugard's ghost —
polished whiskers, blood-stained boots —
was yomping like a born-again hussar.
From the revenge of Keffi to Goose Green
his Empirical philosophy won through...

But so much for history, time for a coup!

FOWL SELLER CAUGHT
WITH WELL DRESSED CROW
'Such initiative and enterprise go make this nation grow'
Mechanibals toss 'spare-part' in a *Flying Coffin* stew
while witch-doctors sell Valium, the chemist
'Toadsfootbrew'

THERE IS NO GOD BUT ALLAH, well,
          only one or two...
NEPA darkens all our lightness in the hot beer queue.
In the hospital the nurses will change dressings, at a price,
while the market mammies haggle over
          sacks of Oxfam rice...

Whali! Dis our Nijeeria goh dead on such Avar-i-i-i-ce!!

So sorry please de Mockracy done gone finish
we get indigenised Lugocracy; that is
the strong plot revolution while the weak
scrub voting fingers and turn another cheek
for HOPE again wears epaulettes and marches
          through the streets:
see how the Bar Beach vultures start to gather for a feast –
General or Statesman; murderer or thief
          TODAY IS ME, TOMORROW IS YOU
Rich man, poor man, beggarman, chief
          DESTINY UNCHANGEABLE, WHY WORRY?

*For contextual notes to 'Lugard's Bridge' see p. 116

CALABASH CARVER, CHAFFE

The knife defines the man, gouged
into his trade by an ancient cicatrice,
The gourd rotates. The knife's designs
are old as tradition, unique as his grasp;
there is the sun always, circle or star

or ribbon of white, and patterns of notches
alike as the days, among which, deftly,
images of the life his existence defends –
the imperious egret, a suckling calf,
the white bull rampant, pizzle erect

his glans much bigger than his head –
for such gourds are the gifts
you present to a bride, saying;
'May your womb swell ripe as this hemisphere
and your milk run white as its flesh.'

He does not examine his work as he carves,
will bargain and joke without pause,
only stopping to slap hard the belly
of the gourd, to show how she's sound
and worthy of his labour's artless price.

TOURIST GUIDE, WEST AFRICA

Welcome to our *African Experience*
where you will see jungle and monkeys
and native village life.
As you know we Africans are full of energy,
and you see how rhythmically our women move,
even with buckets of water on their heads,
and we are very fertile, like the soil –
feel free to photograph
inside the compounds that we pass –
look, there are green monkeys
and here is Uncle John
who will climb a palm nut tree
and let you try his *jungle juice*
and *fire water...* feel free,
feel free, remember, you are on holidays.
When the children shout 'Toubob' and wave
they mean 'Welcome, welcome...
We are very glad to see you here,'
but please don't throw them coins like that –
see how they're wrestling in the dust –
we don't want them to beg.

There are four main tribes in our country
but now we inter-breed and get mixed up.
At our next stop the village women
will perform a ritual dance of welcome,
you can take photographs
and they may ask you to join in,
at the end they will pass round a calabash;
it is part of our tradition,
already they have built a clinic
with your visitors' donations.
So you see you are very welcome.
We Gambians do not believe in colour,

black or white or brown, is all the same,
but don't trust those damn Senegalese,
and our prisons are filled
with foreigners we can't afford to feed.
On the left is our National Stadium
which was built by the Chinese.
The British give education but no money...
Sorry, please.
Well, you see we are back on the tarmac road
so your hotels must be near by,
I hope you have enjoyed your *African Experience*,
any tips will be gratefully received,
I say, any tips will be gratefully received.

ELMINA

stalking the sun-
light, the dun-
geon unbars...
(Kamau Brathwaite, 'Korabra')

Tossing uneasy in my pink-washed
chalet at the Elmina Motel,
big seas and a thunderstorm flashing,
the breeze from the ocean a prize
beyond price in this stifling
season, I dream the unspeakable;
of hereditary complicities
woven in the fibres of this
pale skin I cannot shrug
for all my ethnic ambiguities –
'The Jamaican poet', so many
faces trying not to frown
when this Brown turns out not to be...
'Òyìnbó', 'Bature', 'Obroni' –
always in West Africa
the stranger, no language here
for that West Indian romance
of fellowship. Here everything
is black and white, though things
are rarely quite as they appear.

Elmina,
a depot on the mainline
of humanity's horrors – Auschwitz,
Rwanda, Babi Yar, the killing
fields of history but hardly
recognised by History as we
were taught it in those twilight
suburbs of the Empire,
still those calamine'd scabs

101

across the face of the globe
were medals of honour, something
'we' could be proud of, notwith-
standing our own miseries
and slavery – whatever it might be –
was something 'we' had ended.

Elmina, if we had found it
on a map, was just another
muddy estuary along the Gold
Coast, nowhere, the back of beyond,
behind God's back.

                Maybe
it was that, though legend says
this squat stone fortress, clinging
to its rock was built on holy ground
and *that* god's curse was played out/
paid out down the centuries.
'Amina', in broken Portuguese
the gold-mine's maw or a city
of salt... either way the castle
is still processing its human
cargoes – now 'African-Americans'
"coming back", searching for roots
and reasons
                (complaining that
they have to pay the First World
ticket price when they are *really*
Africans)
                or puzzled whites
on a mystery tour, hoping
retribution won't be paid out
on *their* skins.

But Heritage Site
or tourist trail, who cares –
these castles do good trade in souvenir's –
postcards, badges, tee shirts, pens
(do they have these things at Auschwitz?)
some 'local made' but most imported:
Trade – West Africa is one big
market place – so Adewale says,
and always has been... Trade: some people
here would sell their grandmothers
if they could make a decent profit –
(okay, okay, their neighbours
or their cousins once removed.)
So, sea-salt, souvenirs or slaves –
what's the big deal...?

Hell, let's pass
the buck again, let's play this oldest
of Imperial games, let's blame
the victims... These forts were built
on rented ground, the slave pens
filled by local traders anxious
that their stock should not escape
and steal their profits.

Things here
are never quite as they appear.

Back to that dream...

The scene – Elmina Castle

> *a fat, bald white man,*
> *sweating with each breath,*
> *an English prof*
> *of African letters,*

BA, MA, Ph.D. —
the card his university
has armed him with
proclaims his
titles and authority.
It is his job to be
detached, to have
some understanding
of the wider contexts —
the Renaissance,
the New World,
the mercantile im-
peratives that drive all
our histories...
We see him sceptically
traipsing round the
dungeons and the walls,
emotion dulled by
sun-scorch and
the simple brutality
of stone, indifferent
to the blackmail
of the coffles
and the bones,
all the clichéd
detritus
of inhumanity
that — in the scale
of things — is only
mundane horror,
all seen — and worse —
elsewhere,
The Coliseum
or The Tower,
in Carreg Cennan
or Rose Hall,

but always some-
how sanitised
by History or
its presentation.
Here evil is
oppressive,
is personal,
though he resists
that sentimental
wallowing in guilts
he cannot own.

'Sins of the fathers' perhaps
though not of mine, long
generations gone of rustics,
tradesmen, labourers
who hardly strayed from home
and each endured their unfair
share of pain and exploitation.
But something in my conscience
prickles in this place, too much
like a raw wound in its grim lack
of all embellishments,
the alien fact of these stone walls,
this yard, these dingy passageways
and cells, the 'feeding hatches'
and the cannon balls out in the sun
that 'miscreants' were chained to
through the day. And then that fetid
narrow way out to the sea
where writhing slaves were packed
like maggots in a fisherman's
tray, desperate to escape
this torment into one hell or another.

To imagine them there,
torn between terror and their instinct
for survival..

As a man I quake with the distress of it...

only hear
how our language betrays us
for though "imagination knows
no colour" somehow *I* cannot
enter in *their* heads, *their* faces
do not occupy my dreams...

But who was goading them like beasts
into a pen? Who man-handled them
as cargo on the ships, beat them
to silence below decks?
These
are the men with whom my spirit
knows some awful kinship
defying all disclaimers of complicity.

Three of them come forward in my dream.

1: John Brown – soldier, in the condemned cell
If my fathers had been here
they would have been among
the squaddies, the labourers
press-ganged, conscripted
or driven by their shame
into another life. That class
of men who did what they were told
or took the bloody consequences.

So John Brown
tossed into that stinking hole,
buried alive

for some chance misdemeanour
while all around
brute History unfolds,
is in despair.
He knows, once here, men starve
or rot, or — if in luck —
are just hauled out and hanged,
their bodies left
for vultures on St. Jagoe's Hill.

But confronting
that darkness — now and to come —
he clings to scant hope...
that some whim makes the Governor
pause and relent,
decide merely to have the skin off
his back, have him
march in the sun with full pack
till he drops
or cast off with the blacks to far
Indies... God
how he envied them their lot... He
almost laughed.

Why does my imagination quail
at that one man's degradation
more vividly than it will rage
at the full horror of this place?

2: *John Smith — Trader in slaves*
Or if not the poor accursed squaddie, then
the merchant/middle man who used
this 'House of Trade' to choose which stock

he'd send off to their Caribbean doom.
Perhaps with conscious irony
the Dutch who took this fortress

from the Portuguese, transformed
the Catholic church into a market
where new captives were displayed

for merchants to just pick and choose.
They were not popular, these middle-men,
and some — John Smith — rather than risk

the anger of their sturdy purchases,
preferred to view the market through
two peepholes in the old Confessional...

To stand — where he stood — now
and watch, unseen, black tourists
shuffling through the castle tour

is suddenly to be aware of blame
we all *must* share whose civilisation's
grouted by such mean transactions,

the triangle stamped in blood
that brands us down the generations.

Skulking out of the confessional

he's noticed by a party of black pilgrims —
playing their parts/breaking their hearts
whose ancestors may once have borne

John Smith's pale gaze. Their wry,
disdainful, head-shake smiles
condemn him absolutely to his skin

however much he would disclaim,
explain or empathise.

Understand
John Smith and all his kind

as 'men of their time'
who could not have been otherwise
and lived, who had families

and lives elsewhere
and could be kind to horses
and to kids,

who were caught up in a game
they could not comprehend
or change, even had they

wanted to. Does that sound lame?
My fellow-travellers
from the USA might well say so,

if such excuses weren't beneath disdain.
Understand him in his time?
Okay,

but who the Hell cares anyway –
there's no forgiving,
no withholding of the blame

that they can say –
just outrage, anguish
and that simple, elegiac pain.

3. John Jones – Governor of Elmina
It's not the slave gates
or the auction block
or the feeding hatches

where the swill was slopped
that most offends
the tourists passing through.

Rather it's the women's
dungeon block,
an ugly courtyard, set apart,
where female slaves
were 'exercised'
from time to time
and overlooked
from balconies
outside the Governor's rooms.

Some days he'd choose
a lucky wench
to 'visit', as the tour guide says.
A ladder through
the floor of his apartment
was let down and then
the squaddies pushed
the chosen wretches through.

Of course she may have
clambered willingly enough,
swapped one hell for the next,
and clutched, again,
at that faint hope of a reprieve.
If she delivered up
a child pale-skinned enough
the Governor could own it
then, the custom was,
both mother and her babe
were let go free....

It is John Jones who really haunts me:

Gentleman, Governor,
lover of fine wine and poetry,
ambitious now for better things,
aware of Elmina's value
in the Empirical machine
but fearful too, in his dreams,
forever alert for signals
of incipient rebellion,
in no doubt where his head
would lie if the slaves rose up
or the town were to decide
this grim trade
was no longer to its liking.

He bore responsibilities
and maybe in his mind
they justified
his job's few perks —
good wine, good food,
the spacious bedroom
set to catch the breeze,
and then the pick
of these poor wretches:
nubile, svelte,
sometimes unwilling —
fulfilling all his
darkest fantasies.

But proving, too,
that the excusers lied,
he knew these people
were not of some
'lesser breed',

these women
satisfied a need
beyond mere lust
or his delight
in the extravagance
of power — poor John Brown
rotting in his stinking
cell below. Their bodies
spoke to something soft
within himself, a
dangerous emotion
in this time and place —
something like sorrow
or apology, that
needs must be suppressed.

It is that weakness
which makes him most vivid
now: unwilling to deny
himself those dangerous
pleasures. Beyond fear
and duty and, even here,
his moral scruples,
when it was gifted
on a plate like that,
he took it —
                as I'm quite
certain I'd have done.

And if like him in that,
why not the rest?

            Come on,
        we're talking genocide here,
        Middle Passage, mutilation,
        rape, such cruelties

there are no words to say...
and you, old Mr. Softee,
who now debates the rights
and wrongs of standing on
the cockroaches infesting
your bathroom ...

But the truth is
I'd have done it all, taken
whatever chance was my life's
haul and not worried over much
about morality or justice
or the law. Does that make me
a monster? Would history
excuse me too? And where's
the line? If I'd be John Jones
here why not the Commandant
of Auschwitz? If, really,
I must choose between
my skin and some poor Other's
– pre-destined it would seem
to play the victim
in our cyclic inhumanity –
are there some things I
wouldn't do...?

That's
where the horror of Elmina is
for me: beyond the
unspeakable fate of the slaves
and the comfort blanket
of a generalised rage
that is the blame of race
complicity, beyond
the stench and contagion
and the shame of all our

histories... it is this
stripping away of the sham
that is my nineteen-nineties
irony, my professional
detachment, my sneering,
shrugging, man-of-the-world-
machismo that has
seen it all before and asks
'what else would you expect'
which means, 'what else
would you expect from them....'

John Brown, John Smith, John
Jones, familial ghosts
who prove I am no stranger here
where everything is black
and white, though things are
never quite as they appear.

A CANDLE FOR KEN SARO-WIWA

How untell the lies / How pray for forgiveness
when the departed made wise / Demand restitution?
Ken Saro-Wiwa 'Songs in a Time of War'

I have it in my conference folder still
pointing its waxy finger of accusation
wrapped in the black 'solidarity' ribbons
we all wore – which soon became our flags of mourning.
But then no one believed that they would do it, really,
it was all show, the huff and bluff and puffery
of soldier boys flexing their rifles, fondling their balls.

And the theatre was so hot, the air-conditioning long gone
and the actors had been held up on the road,
and then eventually the play was just so static, and so long...
And man, I'd come five thousand miles the night before,
I hadn't slept, I had a headache and jet lag...
I felt I had excuse enough to creep out of the show
before the midnight vigil planned for Ken Saro-Wiwa,

the candlelight parade, the songs, the cussing out and cursing,
pretending threats then pleading Human Rights.
And though I know it didn't make one smut of difference –
those bastards had him stitched up long ago –
that if Mandela and Bill Clinton and the Pope
couldn't change their minds then my brief candle
in that crowd would hardly show...

but still it hurts me now to find it here, unlit,
a prayer not sent, unheard by whichsoever god
might just have intervened... But that's just shit,
self-serving guilt and sentiment that Sozaboy
for freedom would have scorned. Let me no lie, you sabe?
It wasn't candles that he needed, or false prayers
but what he's got – our outrage, our compassion, our contempt.

I hope this poem works without these notes but the experience and culture that inspired it will be strange to most readers and the notes are just meant to make some of the more obscure references more accessible.

p. 88 'Lugard's Bridge': Frederick Lugard was Governor of Nigeria from 1912 to 1919. Prior to that he had seen military service in India, Sudan, Burma, Uganda and Nyasaland. Then in 1894 he took a post with the Royal Niger Company and in 1900 he was made High Commissioner for Northern Nigeria. He instigated the policy of 'indirect rule', an apparently benign form of imperialism which, none-the-less, radically distorted the political culture of northern Nigeria.

Lugard's Bridge is the small suspension bridge that crossed the Niger at his administrative headquarters at Zungeru, across which he and all his officials must have walked when setting out for their tours of duty in the north. In the poem it is also the way that all contemporary British expatriates working in Nigeria 'enter' the country. It has been moved to Kaduna where it is preserved, more or less, as an historical relic.

p. 88 'Africa beyond reach... ': Jean Paul Sartre in his introduction to the early anthology of African writing, *Orphée Noir*.

p. 88 'Take up the White Man's Burden': from Rudyard Kipling's poem of that title.

p. 88 'Zungeru': Lugard's Administrative Headquarters when he was High Commissioner for Northern Nigeria.

p. 88 'ADOs': Assistant District Officers.

p. 89 'Harmattan': the wind that blows dust and 'cold' south from the Sahara every year.

p. 90 'Shakespeare/quinine and the Trinity': although the policy of Lugard was to allow/encourage local religions, inevitably the culture and values of the colonisers *infected* the indigenous cultures.

p. 91 'leaning on an oilbean': Christopher Okigbo, 'The Passage' from *Heavensgate*.

p. 91 'Flying Pigeon': a cheap and very popular brand of pedal cycle in Nigeria, made in China.

p. 92 'honoured with his thumb': all parcels going through the Nigerian postal system have to be tied with string and sealed with sealing wax.

p. 93 'Picasso's D'Avignon': 'Les Demoiselles d'Avignon' was Picasso's first cubist painting, borrowing images from African art.

p. 93 'Sweet Destiny': the fundamentalist Muslim, and Christian, belief that everything that happens to an individual is God's Will so that human ambition or human precautions taken in, for example, the way they drive, is a kind of heresy.

p. 93 'ghastly accident': every other death recorded in the Bereaved columns of Nigerian newspapers seemed to be the result of a "ghastly accident".

p. 93 'Next-Tomorrow': the bureaucratic formula for 'I haven't done it yet, come back another time'. If an official is out of his office, he is 'not on seat'.

p. 94 'Dash': a tip, or more sinisterly and on a grander scale, a bribe.

p. 95 'LEFT HAND, GO SLOW. OH GOD HELP US': like 'No Condition is Permanent', 'There is no God but Allah', 'Today is Me, Tomorrow is You' and 'Destiny Unchangeable, Why Worry' are all

Mammy Wagon slogans; charms or statements of faith that decorate the main form of public transport.

p. 95 'Chop': eat.

p. 96 'WAWA': a colonial fetish, 'explanation' of the way Nigerian reality tended to subvert English/colonial intentions - West Africa Wins Again.

p. 96 'Revenge of Keffi to Goose Green': During Lugard's 'reign' an expeditionary force was sent up country to Keffi to avenge the murder of a British agent – a whole village and the best part of a culture was decimated. Goose Green was of course the site of the battle on the Falkland Islands which demonstrated that those same Empire values persisted in the psyche of the Thatcher government. The Falklands conflict took place while I was living in Nigeria.

p. 96 'FOWL SELLER CAUGHT...': a typically 'poetic' headline from the Nigerian popular press.

p. 96 *Flying Coffin*: the gruesome nickname given to the fast cross-country taxis that, too often, provide a quick route to the afterlife.

p. 97 'NEPA': The Nigerian Electrical Power Agency, though the initials are said to stand for 'Never Eny Power Again'.

p. 97 'Scrub voting fingers': in Nigerian elections the voters are made to dip their fingers in indelible ink as a way of ensuring that they don't vote twice.

p. 97 'Bar Beach': the notorious Lagos beach, site of many public executions.